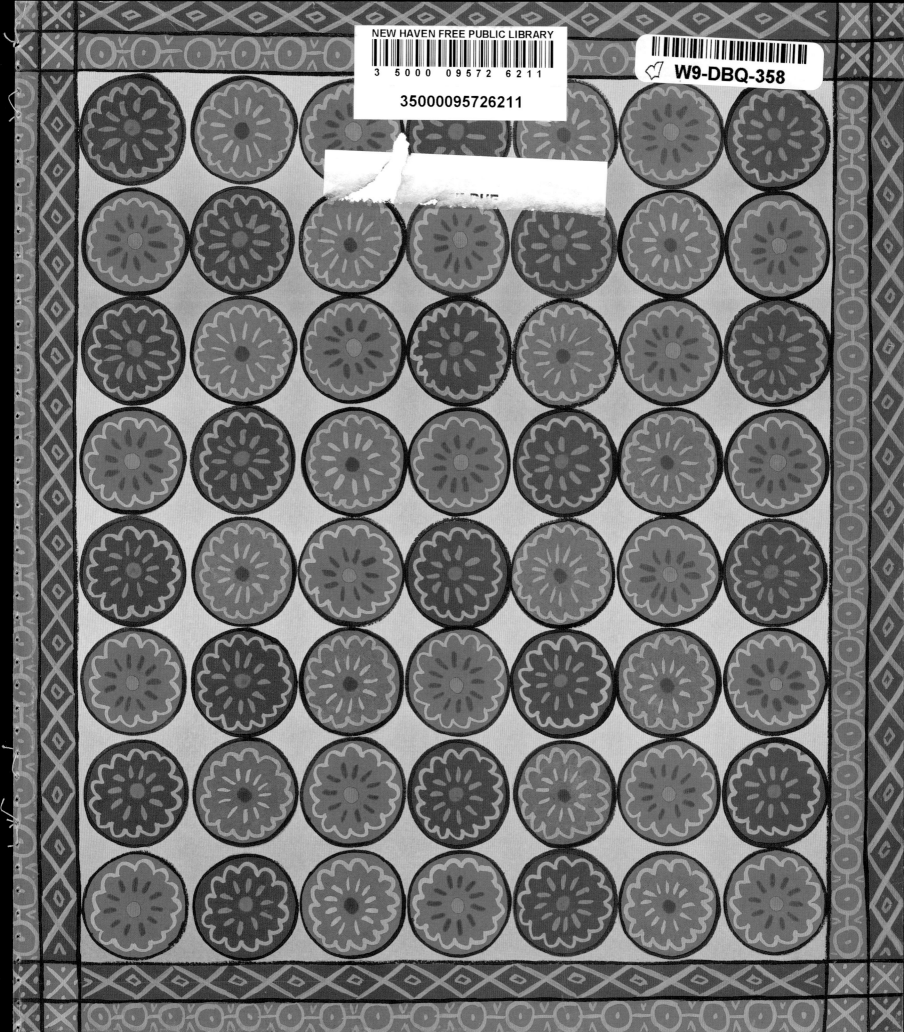

To my family, for their encouragement and joie de vivre
—R. K.

To Rosemary, who introduced me to Paris
—J. M.

First published in the United States of America in September 2010 by Bloomsbury Books for Young Readers
www.bloomsburykids.com

For information about permission to reproduce selections from this book, write to
Permissions, Bloomsbury BFYR, 175 Fifth Avenue, New York, New York 10010

Paintings based on *Mona Lisa* by Leonardo da Vinci. 1503–1506. Oil on poplar wood, 53 x 77 cm. Louvre Museum, Paris.

Library of Congress Cataloging-in-Publication Data
Knapp, Ruthie.
Who stole Mona Lisa? / by Ruthie Knapp ; illustrations by Jill McElmurry.
p.   cm.
Summary: Tells the story of the famous Leonardo da Vinci portrait known as the *Mona Lisa*, including its 1911 theft from the Louvre in Paris,
from the point of view of the subject of the painting. Includes an author's note with facts about the painting.
ISBN 978-1-59990-058-2 (hardcover) • ISBN 978-1-59990-549-5 (reinforced)
1. Leonardo, da Vinci, 1452–1519. Mona Lisa—Juvenile fiction. [1. Leonardo, da Vinci, 1452–1519. Mona Lisa—Fiction. 2. Art thefts—Fiction.]
I. McElmurry, Jill, ill. II. Title.
PZ7.K727Wh 2010   [E]—dc22   2010005512

Illustrations created using gouache on 140-lb cold-pressed watercolor paper
Typeset in Guardi and P22 Cruz Brush Pro
Book design by Donna Mark

Printed in China by Hung Hing Printing (China) Co., Ltd., Shenzhen, Guangdong
2 4 6 8 10 9 7 5 3 1 (hardcover)
2 4 6 8 10 9 7 5 3 1 (reinforced)

All papers used by Bloomsbury Publishing, Inc., are natural, recyclable products made from wood grown in
well-managed forests. The manufacturing processes conform to the environmental regulations of the country of origin.

WHO STOLE
Mona Lisa?

Ruthie Knapp

ILLUSTRATED BY
Jill McElmurry

BLOOMSBURY

NEW YORK BERLIN LONDON

Here they come.

People with up hair. People with down hair.
People with skirts. People with shirts.
People with hats and spats, boots and suits.

They are coming to stare at me, *Mona Lisa*.

Shhh. . . . Let's listen to the guide.

"This is *Mona Lisa*! The mighty *Mona Lisa*.
The greatest painting in the world.
She is famous for her mysterious smile.
Is it a growing smile or a knowing smile?
A shy smile or a sly smile?

Now look at her eyes. They follow you wherever you go."

Everyone moves.
Some walk to the left. Some walk to the right.
Some stoop low. Some stand on their tippy-toes.
Children turn sideways and sometimes upside down
to peek through their legs.

"Is that *Mona Lisa*?" they ask. "Is she real?"
Tall people poke their noses up close.
I can smell their breath: garlic, coffee, cigars.
They all stare at me.

Shhh. Here's the guide again.

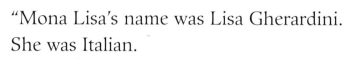

"Mona Lisa's name was Lisa Gherardini.
She was Italian.
She married when she was sixteen.
'Mona' means 'my lady' in Italian.

"Mona Lisa got tired posing for her portrait.
When she squirmed, the painter told her to be still.
If she dozed, he tickled her nose with his brush.
If she scratched, he asked if she had ants in her pants!
When Mona was moody, he hired musicians and clowns to amuse her."

Leonardo da Vinci is the artist who painted me.
It took him four years!
Leonardo loved me.
He looked at me while he ate pasta.
He would not travel without me.
He said I was his masterpiece.

I was famous because Leonardo was famous.
Fans jammed his studio to watch him paint.
Sometimes he set off colored smoke bombs to please them.
"Oooh, ahhh! Amazing," they said.

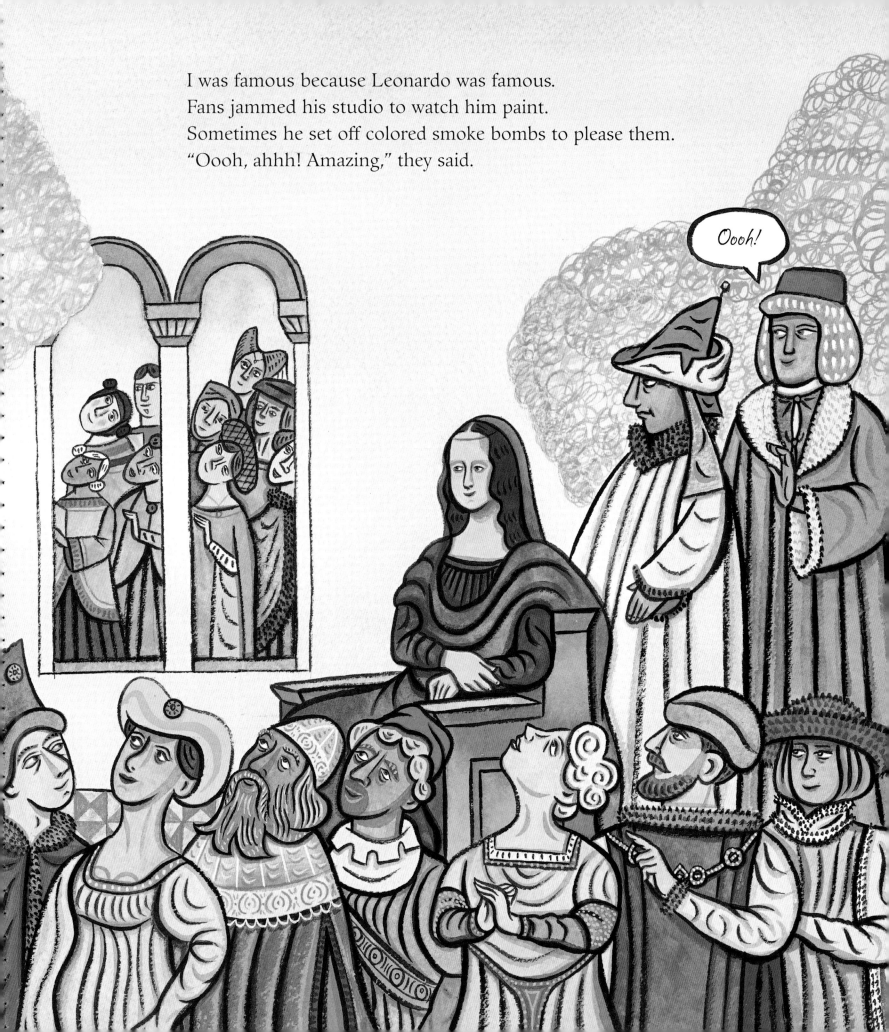

Leonardo was a sculptor, an architect, an inventor, and an engineer.
He drew designs of helicopters, parachutes, tanks, and a robot.
People heard he wrote backward. DRAWKCAB!? How clever is that?
People heard he loved animals. They had seen him buy animals in cages
at the market, only to set them free.

And people saw he was an amazing painter.
Soon I was the most famous painting in Europe.
I was famous for being famous.

A French king named François the First invited Leonardo to paint in his court, and the two men became friends. After Leonardo died, I was given to King François, who admired me as he feasted on frog legs and wine. I stayed in France for many years with many different kings: two named François, three named Henri, one Charles, and four Louis.

Finally, a French emperor named Napoleon got me. Napoleon hung me in his bedroom. He looked at me as he dusted the diamonds in his crown. One day, he decided to give me to the Louvre Museum in Paris, where I could be seen by the world.

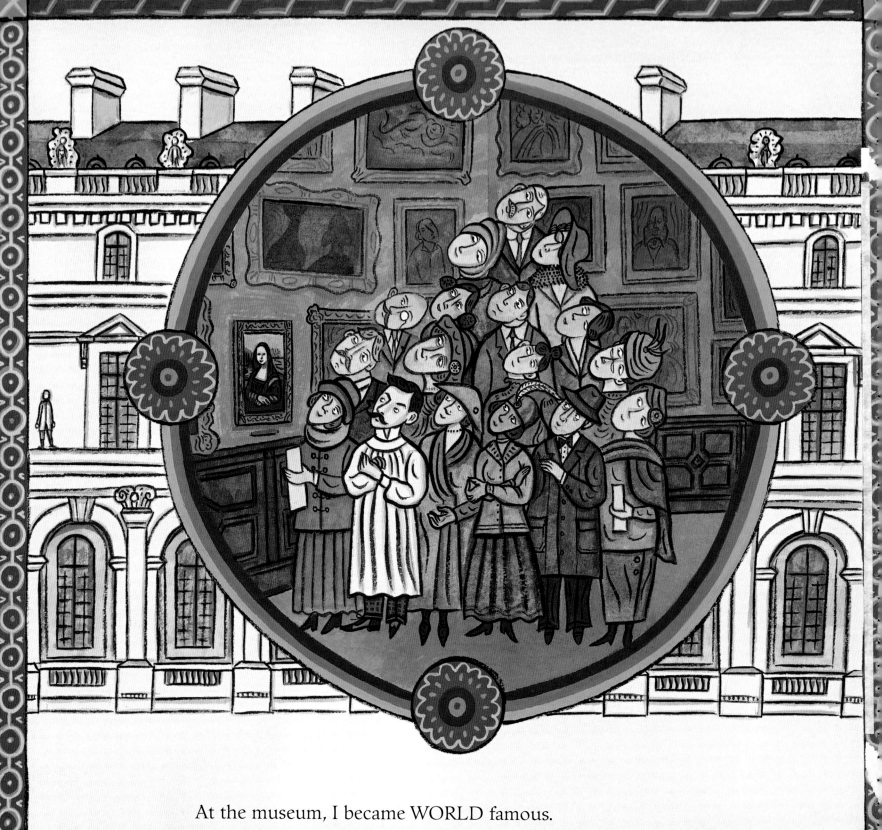

At the museum, I became WORLD famous.
Day after day, crowds came to see me.
Day after day, a man with a mustache came to look at me too.

One hot night in August, I heard footsteps. The man with the mustache came alone in the dark. He measured me: 21 inches wide by 30 inches tall. Then he tiptoed away. Early the next morning, I heard footsteps again. The man with the mustache was back. This time, he was wearing a white workman's smock. He looked behind him, then he raised both hands and ripped me off the wall. Ouch!

First I lurched sideways, then upside down. I felt sick.
My veil slid over one eye. A honey cake fell from my lap.
He hid me under his white smock.
I could feel his heart beat, *da dump, da dump!*
He tiptoed to a dark place and pried me from my frame.
Eeech! His shoes squeaked as he sneaked out of the museum.

The next day, the museum went wild. Where was the *Mona Lisa*? Where was the most famous painting in the world? Did someone hide her?

They looked for me in closets and corners.
They looked in dustbins and vents.
They found a fingerprint and my frame in a stairwell.
Aha! She must be in the photo studio!
But I was not.

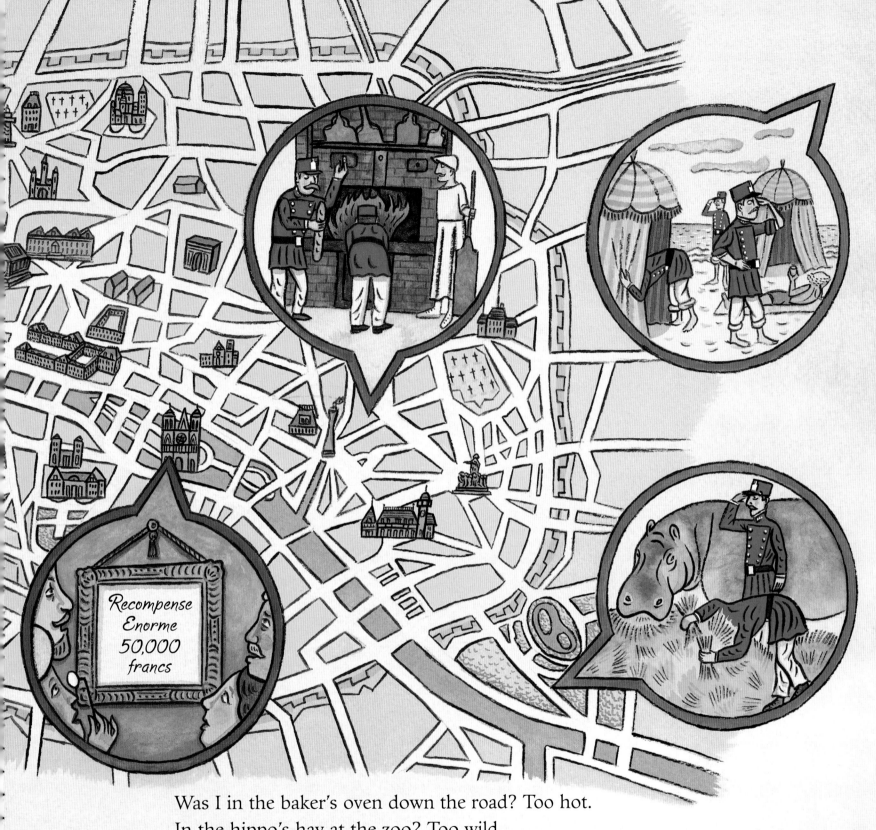

Was I in the baker's oven down the road? Too hot.

In the hippo's hay at the zoo? Too wild.

In the cheese shop? Too smelly.

Detectives searched boats and beaches, freight trains and farms.

The museum posted a reward for my return.

They asked fortune-tellers to track me down.

Still, people came to see No Mona. Millions of people.

People from near and people from far.

People from Giza, people from Pisa.

People from New York and Peking.

Some of them cried. One fainted with grief.

All that was left of me was a space on the wall. People still came.

They came to see the hooks where I hung.

They wanted to see where I WASN'T.

They wrote me poems and songs. They sent me love letters.

The man with the mustache loved me too.
He said I reminded him of someone special.
He looked at me at every meal:
over apples, eggs, and trout;
cake and prunes and piglet snout.
He looked at me on rainy days, on snowy days,
and during summer squalls.

He looked at me when he bathed.
He looked at me while he shaved.
He looked at me for TWO years.
I was tired of the man with the mustache.
I missed my wall.
I missed people staring.
I missed children looking sideways and upside down.

One day the man with the mustache heard the police were searching
for me nearby. He grabbed me and stuck me under the stove.
I could hardly breathe.

I thought of my kings in their beautiful palaces.
I thought of the museum and my place on its wall.
I remembered when I was the great *Mona Lisa*.
Now, instead of crowds, I saw cobwebs.
Instead of admirers, ants.

The man with the mustache decided it was not safe to keep me in Paris. He wrapped me in red cloth, stuffed me in a trunk, and took me back to Italy by train. The train screeched around bends and roared through tunnels. Heavy things bumped my trunk as the man with the mustache growled and cursed.

When we arrived in Italy, he tried to sell me, but people recognized me and called the police. The man with the mustache was sent to jail, and I was booked on an express train back to Paris . . .

. . . where I was returned to my wall at the museum.

The museum went wild. Everyone was talking. "*Mona Lisa* is back!"
People brought me flowers and cried with joy. They lit fireworks.
Did I look the same? Was I hurt?

People lined the streets to see me.
100,000 people visited me on my first day back.
Suddenly I was fashionable. Women tried to smile like me
and wore cosmetics to color their skin like mine.

Now you know why I am smiling. I am happy to see you.
I am happy to be back where I belong. I am happy to be me, *Mona Lisa*.
But mine is a knowing smile. It has stored secrets for more than 500 years.
The secrets of artists and kings, a hot night in August, and a mustache.
It is a smile that knows many secrets, but now so do you.

Shhh. . . . Listen to the guide. She's still talking about me.

Author's Note

Leonardo da Vinci (1452–1519) was one of the great painters of the Italian Renaissance. He painted the *Mona Lisa* between 1503 and 1506. In Italy, the *Mona Lisa* is called "La Gioconda," after her husband, Francesco del Giocondo. In France she is known as "La Joconde."

Leonardo achieved Mona Lisa's mysterious smile using a painting technique called *sfumato*. Meaning "softened line," this process creates a smoky effect by blending light tones into darker ones and allowing one form to merge with another without hard outlines.

The *Mona Lisa* was stolen in August 1911 by Vincenzo Perugia, an Italian housepainter and carpenter who worked for a firm responsible for placing Louvre masterpieces under glass. He spent three weeks making a protective glass cover for the *Mona Lisa*.

Seven months later, Perugia returned to the museum and hid in a closet overnight. Early the next day, when the museum was closed to the public, Perugia, dressed in a white Louvre workman's smock, stole the *Mona Lisa*.

Perugia hid her for two years under his stove in a rooming house one mile from the museum. He claimed he stole the *Mona Lisa* to return her to Italy, where she was painted.

After serving a brief jail sentence in Florence, Perugia returned to his hometown in Italy. Seven years later, he moved back to Paris, where he opened a paint shop.

Today, 80 percent of annual visitors to the Louvre come *only* to see the *Mona Lisa*.

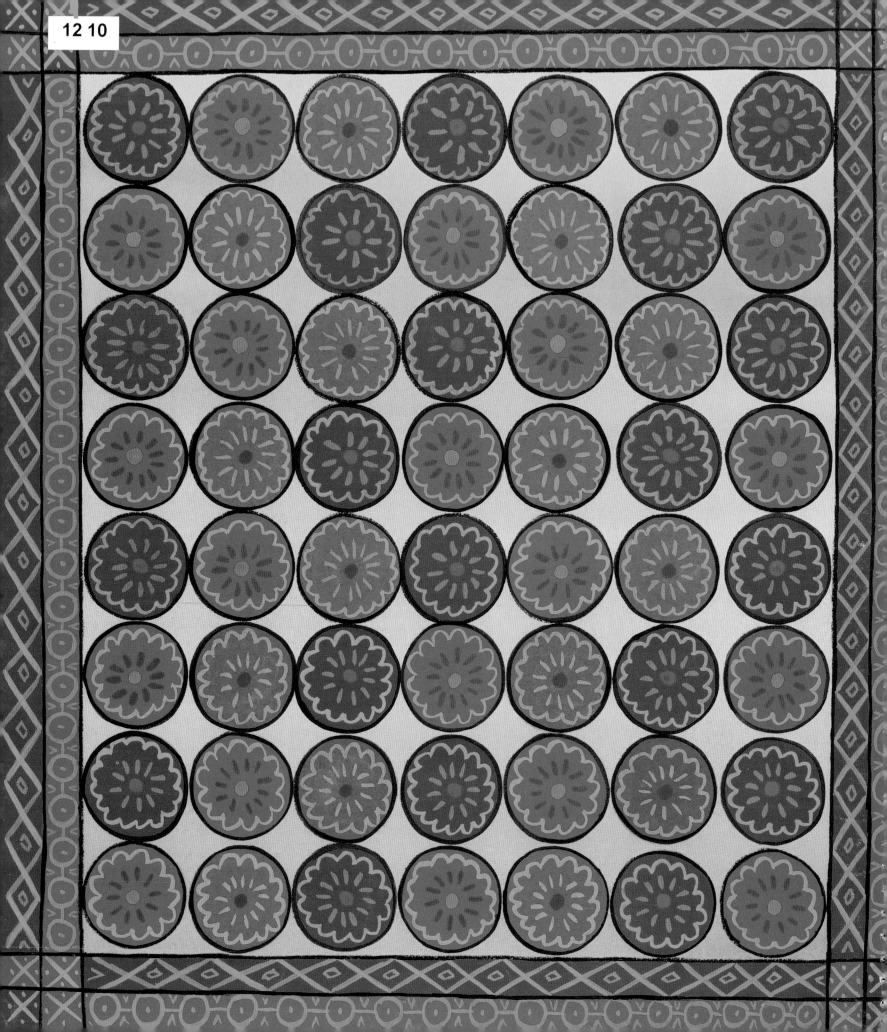